W9-ANN-213

Six Legged World

AMAZING INSECTS

Lynn M. Stone

The Rourke Book Company, Inc.
Vero Beach, Florida 32964

PHOTO CREDITS
© James P. Rowan: cover, p, 20;
© J. H. "Pete" Carmichael: title page, p, 4, 12, 13, 15, 19;
© Lynn M. Stone: p. 7, 8; © James H. Robinson: p. 11, 16

EDITORIAL SERVICES
Janice L. Smith for Penworthy Learning Systems

Library of Congress Cataloging-in-Publication Data

Stone, Lynn M.
    Amazing insects / Lynn M. Stone.
        p. cm. — (Six legged world)
    ISBN 1-55916-309-7
    1. Insects—Juvenile literature. [1. Insects.] I. Title.

QL467.2 .S787 2000
595.7—dc21

00–036932

Printed in the USA

CONTENTS

AMAZING INSECTS

Insects aren't big, and they aren't very smart, at least in human terms. Many of them lead amazing lives.

For instance, try to find a katydid in a Central American rain forest. Certain katydids are among the insects with **cryptic** coloring. They have the same color as the plants around them! Some insects even have the same shape as the vines, leaves, or twigs in which they live. Look at a walkingstick insect – if you can find it.

This amazing katydid in Ecuador mimics a decaying leaf.

The list of amazing insects is endless. There are insects that taste with their feet. Others hear through hairs on their bodies. And many insects have jobs in nature not unlike human jobs. There are insect garbage collectors, herders, workers, and queens. There are soldiers, bodyguards, trappers, travelers, dancers, and **mimics**.

Walkingsticks use their shape and color to nearly disappear among sticks.

AMAZING HONEYBEES

It's not honey that makes honeybees amazing. Honey is basically just bee food that humans happen to like.

It's how honeybees live that's amazing. In the first place, they're among the few animals that work together. Honeybees are **social**. But many social animals simply live or nest together.

Honeybees, in contrast, have organized lives. They divide their work. The main job of so-called worker bees is to find food.

Honeybees swarm at their honeycomb. Honeybees are social insects, like ants.

Workers leave the hive and fly to flowers. The bees suck liquids from the flowers and later make honey from them.

When a worker returns to the bees' home, or hive, it brings the flowers' smell. That helps other workers know what kind of flowers to look for when they leave the hive.

A returning worker may also "dance." Its movements seem to show the other workers the direction and distance of the flower patch.

A honeybee carries pollen on the brushy rear legs. The common honeybee's habits make it one of the most amazing insects.

Amazing monarchs travel up to 3,000 miles (4,800 kilometers) from Canada to reach their winter home in central Mexico.

The tropical tortoise beetle is one of several insects with amazing looks.

13

AMAZING ANTS

Fire ants bite like little terriers. Carpenter ants eat wooden house beams like they are popsicles. Ants aren't on anyone's valentine list. But there are some pretty amazing **species**, or kinds, of ants. Some can lift 50 times their body weight. That's like an 80-pound (36-kilogram) person lifting a Cadillac.

Leaf-cutter ants are amazing, too. Leaf-cutter ants haul leaf clippings to their underground nests. Worker ants ride atop some of the leaves as bodyguards. Their job is to protect the leaf carriers from attack by certain flies.

Leaf-cutter ants haul leaf pieces to their underground den.

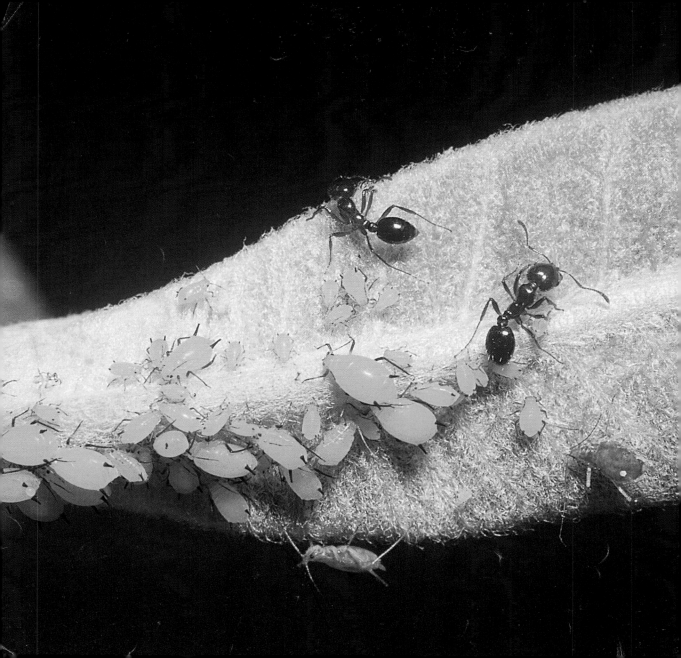

In the nest, tiny worker ants chew the leaves into paste. They add the leaf paste to gardens of **fungus** in the nest. The paste helps the fungus grow. And the ants eat the fungus!

Another type of amazing ant uses aphids for food – without eating them. Aphids are small, plant-eating insects. They release a sweet liquid called honeydew that ants love. Aphids put honeydew on leaves. The ants suck it from the leaves as well as from the aphids themselves. But the ants don't hurt the aphids. In fact, the ants defend the aphids from attackers. Sometimes the ants even shelter the aphids in the ants' underground homes!

Ants tend aphids for the liquid honeydew that aphids produce and ants love.

OTHER AMAZING INSECTS

The 17-year cicada has an amazing life. The cicada hatches from an egg and burrows into the soil. It lives on the threadlike roots of plants – for 17 years! Then the cicada crawls above ground and rapidly changes into a winged adult. But just six weeks later the cicada has mated, laid eggs, and died.

The conehead katydid of Costa Rica protects itself with a swordlike horn and looks that could scare King Kong!

Migrations are long journeys that certain animals make each year, usually in fall and spring. The monarch butterfly's migration is no less than amazing.

Monarchs from as far north as southern Canada travel south each fall. They fly up to 3,000 miles (4,800 kilometres) to a place in Mexico none of them has ever seen.

After 17 years underground in its larva stage, the cicada becomes an adult and lives for about a month.

The monarch is the champion insect traveler. But, the human flea is the champion insect jumper. The tiny flea can jump eight inches (20 centimeters) in an upward direction. This is higher than any other animal can jump in proportion to its size.

GLOSSARY

cryptic (KRIP tik) — that which hides or conceals, such as certain colors or shapes

fungus (FUN gus) — any one of certain simple, plantlike growths

migration (mi GRAY shun) — a long seasonal journey that certain animals undertake year after year

mimic (MIH mik) — to copy the actions or appearance of another; one who copies another

social (SO shul) — being in the company of others

species (SPEE sheez) — within a group of closely related animals, such as butterflies, one certain type (**monarch** butterfly)

FURTHER READING

Find out more about amazing insects and insects in general with these helpful books and information sites:

- Everts, Tammy and Kalman, Bobbie. *Bugs and Other Insects*. Crabtree, 1994
- Green, Jen. *Learn About Insects*. Lorenz, 1998
- Rowan, James P. *Honeybees*. Rourke, 1993
- Stone, Lynn M. *Remarkable Flight of the Monarchs*. Rourke, 1991

Insects on-line at www.letsfindout.com/bug
Wonderful World of Insects on line at www.insect-world.com

INDEX